FAVORITE FOOTBALL TEAMS

NEW ENGLAND PATRIOTS

BY K. C. KELLEY

THE CHILD'S WORLD®

1980 Lookout Drive • Mankato, MN 56003-1705
800-599-READ • www.childsworld.com

ACKNOWLEDGMENTS

The Child's World®: Mary Berendes, Publishing Director
Shoreline Publishing Group, LLC: James Buckley, Jr.,
 Production Director
The Design Lab: Kathleen Petelinsek, Design;
 Gregory Lindholm, Page Production

PHOTOS

Cover: Focus on Football
Interior: AP/Wide World: 9, 17, 18, 22, 23, 25 (Gostowski);
 Focus on Football: 5, 6, 10, 13, 21, 25 (Moss and Brady), 27

Published in the United States of America.

LIBRARY OF CONGRESS
CATALOGING-IN-PUBLICATION DATA

Kelley, K. C.
 New England Patriots / by K.C. Kelley.
  p. cm. — (Favorite football teams)
 Includes bibliographical references and index.
 ISBN 978-1-60253-316-5 (library bound : alk. paper)
 1. New England Patriots (Football team)—Juvenile literature.
I. Title. II. Series.
 GV956.N36K45 2009
 796.332'640974461—dc22   2009009066

TABLE OF CONTENTS

Go, Patriots!

"Three cheers for the red, white, and blue!" People cheer like this for the American flag. They also cheer like this for the New England Patriots! The team's colors are red, white, and blue. Over the past 10 years, the Patriots have been one of the best teams in pro football. They have won three **Super Bowls**! Some of their players are the best and most famous in the National Football League (NFL). Let's meet the Patriots!

Here come the Patriots! Star quarterback Tom Brady (12) leads the team onto the field. Cheerleaders help the fans root for their favorite team!

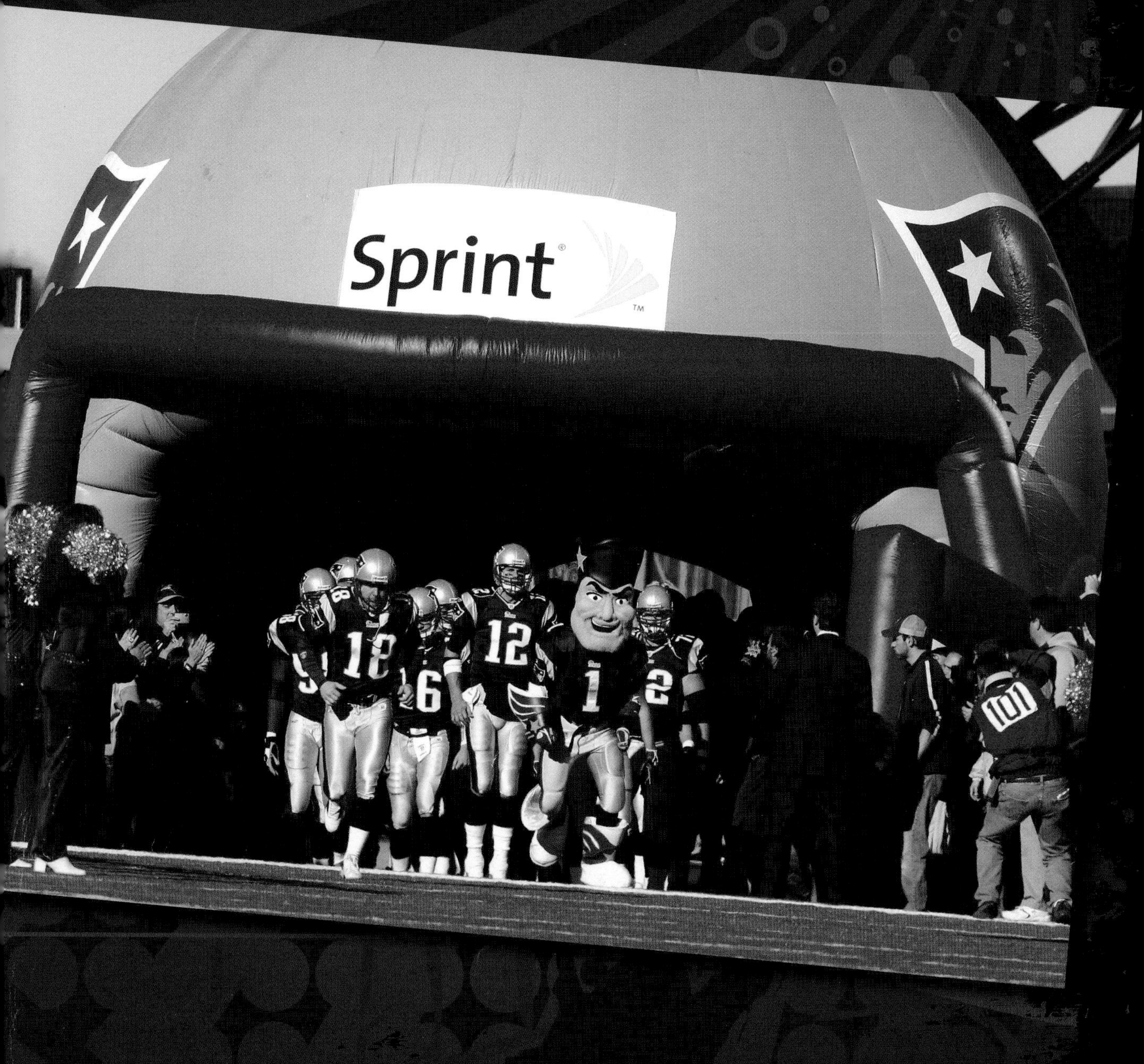
Sprint

Who Are the New England Patriots?

The New England Patriots play in the NFL. They are one of 32 teams in the NFL. The NFL includes the National Football Conference (NFC) and the American Football Conference (AFC). The Patriots play in the East Division of the AFC. The winner of the NFC plays the winner of the AFC in the Super Bowl. The Patriots have been the NFL champions three times!

Shout for joy! That's what Tom Brady (12) is doing. He's happy that teammate Asante Samuel just scored a touchdown for New England.

Where They Came From

The Patriots started in 1960 . . . in another league! The American Football League (AFL) began that year. People started the AFL to compete with the NFL. But the AFL ended up joining the NFL in 1970. At first the Patriots were called the Boston Patriots. They became the New England Patriots in 1971. New England is a large area in the northeastern United States. It includes several states. People in all those states root for the Patriots!

The Patriots used to wear red jerseys. The design on their helmets was different, too. In this game, Jim Plunkett (16) throws a pass down the field.

Who They Play

The Patriots play 16 games each season. There are three other teams in the AFC East. They are the Buffalo Bills, the Miami Dolphins, and the New York Jets. Every year, the Patriots play each of those teams twice. They also play other teams in the NFC and AFC.

It's time to celebrate! The Patriots offense just scored again. This time, the team is playing against the New York Jets, another AFC East team.

Where They Play

The Patriots play their home games at Gillette Stadium. It is in Foxboro, Massachusetts. Foxboro is west of Boston, the state capital. The stadium opened in 2002. Winter weather in Foxboro is often very cold. Gillette Stadium has no roof. Fans and players shiver on cold days. Fans must dress warmly. Even the players sometimes wear knit caps or handwarmers.

Here, the Patriots are playing a night game under the bright lights of Gillette Stadium. Thousands of fans are cheering them on!

13

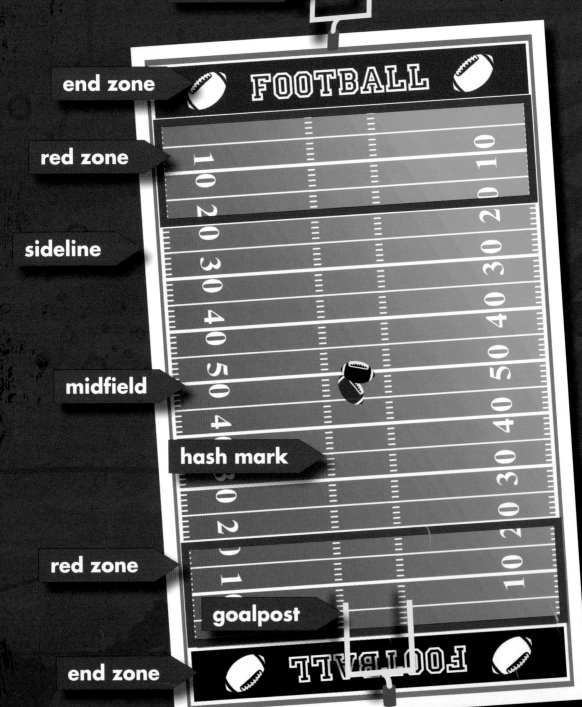

goalpost

end zone

red zone

sideline

midfield

hash mark

red zone

goalpost

end zone

FOOTBALL

The Football Field

An NFL field is 100 yards long. At each end is an **end zone** that is another 10 yards deep. Short white **hash marks** on the field mark off every yard. Longer lines mark every five yards. Numbers on the field help fans know where the players are. Goalposts stand at the back of each end zone. On some plays, a team can kick the football through the goalposts to earn points. During the game, each team stands along one sideline of the field. The field at Gillette Stadium is covered with **artificial**, or fake, grass. Most outdoor NFL stadiums have real grass.

During a game, the two teams stand on the sidelines. They usually stand near midfield, waiting for their turns to play. Coaches walk on the sidelines, too, along with cheerleaders and photographers.

Big Days!

The New England Patriots have had many great moments in their long history. Here are three of the greatest:

1964: The Boston Patriots made it to the AFL Championship Game. But they lost to the San Diego Chargers.

2002: The Patriots won their first Super Bowl. Kicker Adam Vinatieri made a 48-yard **field goal** on the last play of the game! New England beat the St. Louis Rams, 20–17.

2004: Vinatieri did it again! His 41-yard field goal won another Super Bowl. The Patriots topped the Carolina Panthers 32–29.

Colored confetti filled the air after Super Bowl XXXVI. The Patriots won, thanks to a great play by their star kicker.

Tough Days!

The Patriots can't win all their games. Some games or seasons don't turn out well. The players keep trying to play their best, though! Here are some painful memories from Patriots history:

1986: The Patriots finally made it to the Super Bowl—then they got crushed! The Chicago Bears whomped them, 46-10.

1990: The Patriots had their worst season. They won only one of their 16 games!

2008: Star quarterback Tom Brady hurt his knee . . . in the first game of the season! He didn't play again until 2009.

The first game of 2008 was also the last game of 2008 for Tom Brady (12). Team trainers helped him off the field after he hurt his knee.

Meet the Fans

Patriots fans come from all over New England. Most of the fans live in Massachusetts. But some live in Maine, New Hampshire, Vermont, and Rhode Island. Those states don't have NFL teams, so they cheer for the "Pats." New England fans have had a lot to cheer about in recent years. At home games, they are led by their **mascot**, Pat Patriot.

Why AFC? These Patriots fans are celebrating another AFC championship. They're also bundled up against the cold New England weather.

AUBURN N.H.

AUBURN N.H.

21

Heroes Then . . .

The first big star for the Patriots was **linebacker** Nick Buoniconti. He played in the 1960s. He was later named to the **Pro Football Hall of Fame**. Quarterback Steve Grogan led the Patriots for 17 years. Guard John Hannah was one of the best ever at his position. He blocked for the Patriots for 13 years (1973–1985). **Cornerback** Mike Haynes is another Hall of Fame player. Speedy and smart, he made 46 **interceptions** in his career.

OCT. 20, 1968
BOSTON PATRIOTS 23
VS.
BUFFALO BILLS – 6

1960s
NICK BUONICONTI
Linebacker

Steve Grogan played for the Patriots from 1975 to 1999. He was a good passer and also a very solid runner.

23

Heroes Now . . .

Tom Brady is one of the best quarterbacks in NFL history. He led the team to three Super Bowl wins in four years! He was the Super Bowl Most Valuable Player (MVP) twice! In 2007, he threw 50 touchdown passes. That's the most ever in one season! One of his favorite **receivers** was Randy Moss. Moss caught 23 touchdown passes in 2007, another record. Kicker Stephen Gostkowski has been among the NFL leaders in points scored.

TOM BRADY
Quarterback

RANDY MOSS
Wide Receiver

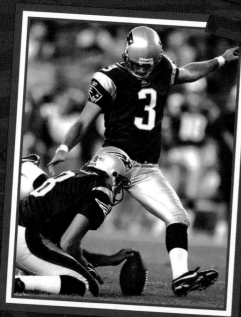

STEPHEN GOSTKOWSKI
Kicker

25

Gearing Up

New England Patriots players wear lots of gear to help keep them safe. They wear pads from head to toe. Check out this picture of linebacker Tedy Bruschi and learn what NFL players wear.

The Football

NFL footballs are made of four pieces of leather. White laces help the quarterback grip and throw the ball. Inside the football is a rubber bag that holds air.

Football Fact

NFL footballs don't have white lines around them. Only college teams use footballs with those lines.

helmet

facemask

shoulder pad

chest pad

gloves

knee pad

cleats

27

FAVORITE FOOTBALL TEAMS

Sports Stats

Note: All numbers are through the 2008 season.

Touchdowns

TOUCHDOWN MAKERS

These players have scored the most touchdowns for the Patriots.

PLAYER	TOUCHDOWNS
Stanley Morgan	68
Ben Coates	50

PASSING FANCY
Top Patriots quarterbacks

PLAYER	PASSING YARDS
Drew Bledsoe	29,657
Steve Grogan	26,886

Quarterbacks

RUN FOR GLORY
Top Patriots running backs

PLAYER	RUSHING YARDS
Sam Cunningham	5,453
Jim Nance	5,323

Running backs

Receivers

CATCH A STAR
Top Patriots receivers

PLAYER	CATCHES
Troy Brown	557
Stanley Morgan	534

TOP DEFENDERS
Patriots defensive records

Most interceptions: Ty Law, 36; Raymond Clayborn, 36
Most **sacks**: Andre Tippett, 100

Defenders

COACH
Most Coaching Wins

Bill Belichick, 116

Coach

Glossary

artificial fake, not real

cornerback a player who covers the other team's receivers and tries to keep them from making catches.

defensive trying to keep the other team from scoring

end zone a 10-yard-deep area at each end of the field

field goal a three-point score made by kicking the ball between the upper goalposts

hash marks short white lines that mark off each yard on the football field

interceptions catches made by defensive players

linebacker a defensive player who begins each play standing behind the main defensive line

mascot a person in costume or an animal that helps fans cheer for a team

offense players who have the ball and are trying to score

Pro Football Hall of Fame the place in Canton, Ohio, that honors the game's greatest players

quarterback the key offensive player who starts each play and passes or hands off to a teammate

receivers offensive players who catch forward passes

running backs offensive players who run with the football and catch passes

sacks tackles of a quarterback behind the line of scrimmage

Super Bowl the NFL's annual championship game

touchdown a six-point score made by carrying or catching the ball in the end zone

Find Out More

BOOKS

Buckley, James Jr. *The Scholastic Ultimate Book of Football.* New York: Scholastic, 2009.

Madden, John, and Bill Gutman. *Heroes of Football.* New York: Dutton, 2006.

Polzer, Tim. *Play Football! A Guide for Young Players from the National Football League.* New York: DK Publishing, 2002.

Savage, Jeff. *Tom Brady.* Minneapolis: Lerner Books, 2008.

Stewart, Mark, and Jason Akins. *The New England Patriots.* Chicago: Norwood House Press, 2006.

WEB SITE

Visit our Web site for lots of links about the New England Patriots and other NFL football teams:

childsworld.com/links

Note to Parents, Teachers, and Librarians: We routinely verify our Web links to make sure they are safe, active sites—so encourage your readers to check them out!

Index

About the Author

K. C. Kelley is a huge football fan! He has written dozens of books on football and other sports for young readers. K. C. used to work for NFL Publishing and has covered several Super Bowls.